Autism Connections

Lots of Ways to Play

Exploring How Friends Interact

Leslie Kimmelman

Lerner Publications ◆ Minneapolis

Alongside friends from *Sesame Street,* children will explore how we all experience the world in unique ways—from developing friendships and flexible thinking to how we communicate and receive support. This series celebrates all children, helping young readers and their grown-ups appreciate the amazing qualities in everyone, fostering greater understanding.

Sincerely,
the Editors at Sesame Workshop

Table of Contents

We Are All Amazing

Friends make life sweeter. Your friends may not like all the same things that you like. They may play in different ways.

But each friend is
unique . . . and amazing.

Many Ways to Play

When making a new friend, sometimes it helps to be patient. You might need to slow down or repeat your words.

Or you may have to
wait for an answer.

Playing side by side can be fun. What drawings or paintings will you make? What will you build?

What games do your friends like? Maybe you can make up a new game together!

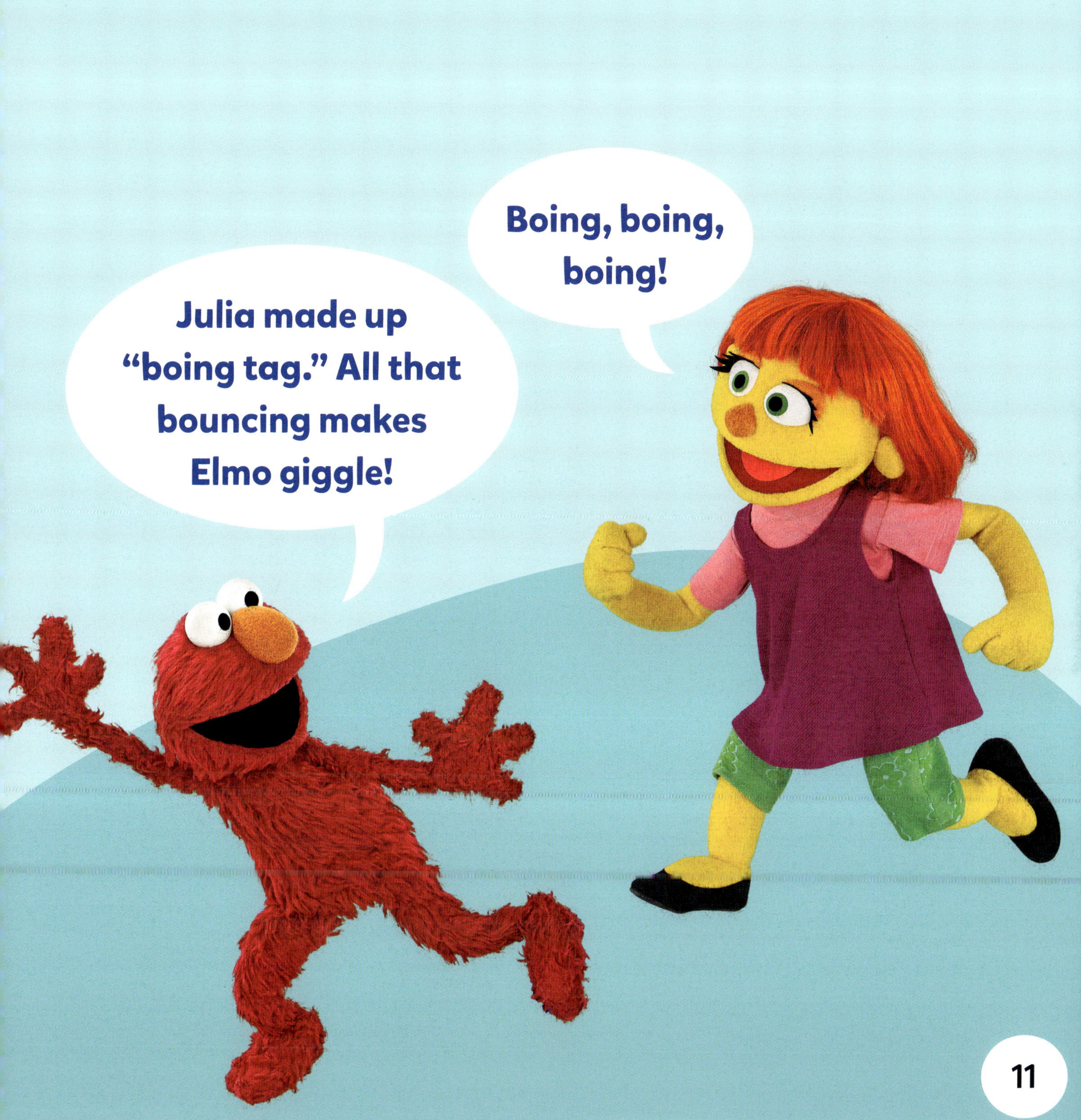
Boing, boing, boing!
Julia made up "boing tag." All that bouncing makes Elmo giggle!

If it gets too loud, some friends may need a break.

I LOVE NOISE!
Too noisy!

Some friends like being in the middle of everything. And some friends may need a little more space.

It's fun for me to play with friends!

Friends can have different ways to show they care about each other. How do you show you care?

We give one
another big
hugs!

Friends are lucky to have each other! You and your friends are all different. You are all amazing.

Friends forever!

Your Turn!

All about Me

On a separate sheet of paper, answer these questions to discover more about yourself. For each question, write down the letter of the answer that is true for you! Ask a friend to answer the questions too, and see how your answers compare. You may include more than one answer to each question. There are no wrong answers!

1. I like to:

A. Play games or do activities in a group
B. Read quietly on my own
C. Paint with a friend

2. I like to be:

A. Off to the side
B. In the middle of everything
C. Playing with one friend at a time

3. To show I'm happy or excited, I:

A. Loudly shout "hooray!"
B. Flap my hands
C. Jump up and down
D. Quietly giggle or smile

Glossary

patient: being able to wait for something

robot: a machine that can do tasks

tag: a game where one player chases other players until they catch someone and it becomes their turn

Read More

Bailey, Jenn. *Henry, Like Always*. Chronicle Books, 2023.

Cook, Jennifer. *My Friend Julia: A Sesame Street® Book about Autism*. Lerner Publications, 2024.

Miller, Connie Colwell. *William Is Loading . . .* Amicus Learning, 2025.

Index

Photo Acknowledgments

Image credits: Ariel Skelley/Getty Images, p. 4; kali9/Getty Images, p. 6; Tashi-Delek/Getty Images, p. 9; wundervisuals/Getty Images, p. 10; FatCamera/Getty Images, p. 12; Amorn Suriyan/Getty Images, p. 14; PeopleImages.com - Yuri A/Shutterstock, p. 16; SolStock/Getty Images, p. 18.

Lerner Publications Company
An imprint of Lerner Publishing Group, Inc.
241 First Avenue North
Minneapolis, MN 55401 USA

For reading levels and more information, look up this title at www.lernerbooks.com.

Main body text set in Mikado a.
Typeface provided by HvD Fonts.

Editor: Annie Zheng **Designer:** Mary Ross
Lerner team: Martha Kranes

Library of Congress Cataloging-in-Publication Data

Names: Kimmelman, Leslie author
Title: Lots of ways to play : exploring how friends interact / Leslie Kimmelman.
Description: Minneapolis, MN : Lerner Publications, [2026] | Series: Sesame street autism connections | Includes bibliographical references and index. | Audience: Ages 4–8 | Audience: Grades K–1 | Summary: "There are lots of ways to play! From playing group games to doing quiet activities together, readers will learn alongside Sesame Street characters about different ways friends can play and interact"– Provided by publisher.
Identifiers: LCCN 2025011126 (print) | LCCN 2025011127 (ebook) | ISBN 9798765685099 library binding | ISBN 9798348029210 paperback | ISBN 9798765698273 epub
Subjects: LCSH: Sesame Street (Television program)—Juvenile literature | Play—Juvenile literature | Friendship—Juvenile literature
Classification: LCC HQ782 .K46 2026 (print) | LCC HQ782 (ebook) | DDC 155.4/18—dc23/eng/20250819

LC record available at https://lccn.loc.gov/2025011126
LC ebook record available at https://lccn.loc.gov/2025011127

Manufactured in the United States of America
1-1011845-54585-5/13/2025